A Quick Guide to
ARCHETYPES &
ALLEGORY

A QUICK GUIDE SERIES

KEN JOHNSON

Heritage
House
Books

Published By:
Heritage House Books, LLC
P.O. Box 263
Milton, FL 32572-0263

www.hhbooks.co

The contents and opinions expressed in this book do not necessarily reflect the views and opinions of Heritage House Books, LLC. Any mentioning of brands or trade names does not constitute any endorsement.

When the author refers to passages in the *Holy Bible*, unless otherwise referenced, no specific translation is being referred to. Instead, the reader is encouraged to read from numerous versions to gain a better understanding of the referenced translated text.

ISBN-13: 978-1-7338333-0-1 (Paperback)
ISBN-13: 978-1-7338333-1-8 (EBook)

Library of Congress Control Number: 2019903907
©2019 by Heritage House Books, LLC

Cover Design & Book Formatting By: Amit Dey
Cover Art By: Engin Akyurt, Michal Jarmoluk, Pete Linforth, and Etienne Marais
under a free commercial use agreement with www.Pixabay.com

Publisher's Cataloging-in-Publication Data
provided by Five Rainbows Cataloging Services

Names: Johnson, Ken, 1977- author.
Title: A quick guide to archetypes & allegory / Ken Johnson.
Description: Milton, FL : Heritage House Books, 2019. | Series: A quick guide.
Identifiers: LCCN 2019903907 | ISBN 978-1-7338333-0-1 (paperback) | ISBN 978-1-7338333-1-8 (ebook)
Subjects: LCSH: Fiction—Authorship. | Fiction—Technique. | Authorship—Handbooks, manuals, etc. | Archetype (Psychology) in literature. | Allegory. | Creative writing. | BISAC: LANGUAGE ARTS & DISCIPLINES / Writing / Authorship. | LANGUAGE ARTS & DISCIPLINES / Writing / Fiction Writing.
Classification: LCC PN3383.C4 J64 2019 (print) | LCC PN3383.C4 (ebook) | DDC 808.3/97--dc23.

To my dearest wife, Toshana,
thank you for your constant
support and wise counsel.

Table of Contents

Prelude

In today's world, the concept of character archetypes, being used as building blocks for evolving characters, and laden with specific allegory, is considered a passé notion in contemporary literary and cinematic circles. In my countless interviews of authors and cinematic leaders, one thing has stuck out – they all reject the idea of using archetypes and allegory in their plots.

Part of the reason for this is a fundamental change in our collective beliefs regarding the subjects of psychology, theology, and philosophy. Now a world of individuals, rather than communities making up grand societies, we reject the belief that humanity's collective unconsciousness is somehow psychologically connected to symbols and icons. We especially reject the notion that such symbols and icons carry with them any latent psychological connotation.

Once great thought leaders, like Carl Jung, are now disapproved of, and even made taboo, in many writing circles. Such early pioneers of this field are now made out to be something akin to astrologists – trying to find meaning out of something where no evidence seems to exist.

Industry professionals would have us to believe everything is written in good fun and with no ulterior motive or associated allegory. Any assertion of hidden meaning is explained away as being coincidental, some marketing-based copycatting of ideas, and the writer's wealth of knowledge being somehow subconsciously converged on the pages in a newly minted form.

Such a posited notion is not innocuous. The emphatic rejection of archetype-based characters, and intrinsically derived allegory, in stories, gives literary and cinematic professionals a certain level of *culpable deniability (plausible deniability)*. For example, a talking donkey, being questionably used in a storyline with other *fairytale creatures*, can easily be attributed to nothing more than a fantasy created by professionals in a pure work of fiction. They can deny any claims that such a character was an archetype relating to the talking donkey in Numbers 22:28-30 and 2 Peter 2:16 of the *Holy Bible*. This way, any questionable use of the talking donkey, say mating with a dragon, can be easily denied as a hidden motive intended to publicly besmirch, ridicule, and mock Judeo-Christian beliefs.

As we'll address later in this book, works, like the 1980s cult classic television series *V*, were initially written one way to talk about real life social issues and perceived threats, only to have executives order the story changed to be about aliens. Why would television executives want to make a story of fascists taking over America into an Earth-based space opera? Could it be that writers would be able to elicit the same concepts of a fascist takeover, while circumnavigating latent socio-political prejudices in audiences, by utilizing the alien archetype to speak to our collective unconsciousness?

Carl Jung, a Swiss psychologist, first posited the notion of a *collective unconscious* over 100 years ago. Jung's psychological concepts were based, at least in part, upon Sigmund Freud's own *archaic remnants* and *primal horde* concepts. In November of 1929, Jung wrote a piece titled, "The Significance of Constitution and Heredity in Psychology," in which he noted how individual persons react to *primordial images*, or *archetypes* as he called them, based upon certain "influences, traditions, and excitations working on the individual, but more often without any sign of them." In other words, without any evidence of a preexisting cause, people tend to react to certain archetypal images in a predictable pattern based upon a series of psychological and anthropological factors.

Later, in October of 1936, Jung lectured to the Abernethian Society in London. Here, Jung further clarified the understanding of the collective unconscious by asserting the collective unconscious is inherited.

In other words, we are genetically predisposed to certain archetypes and the allegory they represent. Many of the very archetypes we have today, Jung would argue, comes from a shared common genetic ancestry.

Why else would the Chinese, the British, and many Native American tribes have dragon-based stories despite being separated by vast oceans, differences in language, and differences in culture? Why then do the Irish, the Cherokee, and the Maori all have stories of magical little people? Yes, it is a bit compelling once religion, proximate location, race, social status, and other factors are all ruled out as possible contributing forces.

After Jung, various experts posited different takes regarding archetypes. Indeed, for a time, character archetypes were taught as fact in colleges and universities. It became understood that these primordial images could change over time. For example, the *Incredible Hulk* is an archetype based upon Robert Louis Stevenson's *Dr. Jekyll and Mr. Hyde*, which is nothing more than a cultural adaptation to the old *werewolf* archetype.

Later, further understandings developed, asserting that our state of being could ignite a deeply profound attraction to certain archetypes. In 1954, the Comic Code Authority was formed based upon this latter notion. As you will learn later on in this book, the CCA did not allow certain archetypes to be played out as characters in American comic books. Ergo, this is why one could not do a comic about a werewolf, but one could do a comic about a man transforming into a hulking monster.

Verily, at the heart of storytelling is where we find the archetype most active and impactful. Sometimes enigmatic and lacking clear derivation, it is powerful and somehow innately known by most people. It's intrinsically as much a part of the human condition as is laughter, tragedy, and triumph over adversity.

In this book, an archetype is best defined as a specific type of *allegory* (hidden meaning) made manifest through a character. Its functional role is to play upon the collective unconsciousness to gain immediate, subconscious acceptance by the reader for a concept or plot.

This psychological shorthand affords writers the ability to move a story along, rather quickly, and without any unnecessary character development. The allegory for the archetypal character can change based upon the age of the targeted audience, the culture of the audience, the writer playing upon the allegories of previously produced works of others now in the public domain, and other considerations.

It's important to note, over time, that there has grown a certain ambiguity regarding what an archetype is and how it functions. For instance, some now confuse archetypes with plots – two entirely different things. Plots are, in their purest form, allegory-rich story concepts, which writers can utilize to develop a plotline. For more information on plots, you should check out my companion book in this series, *A Quick Guide to Plots & Plotlines*.

It should also be made clear; all archetypes fall into two categories: Non-Humanoid and Humanoid. Non-humanoid archetypes are characters like dragons and unicorns. Humanoid archetypes are characters, which appear somewhat human in form like kings, angels, vampires, some aliens, etc.

Almost every continent in the world has a dragon story, a were-animal tale, a vampire story, alien stories, devil stories, etc. Even though these creatures may look drastically different, there is something in the human psyche where we all intuitively, and subconsciously, know the hidden allegory of the archetype being portrayed.

We are even subconsciously driven to gain enjoyment from books, stories, films, etc., involving archetypal characters which we self-identify with a given character type. One finds this especially true in monster-based stories where the creature is a portrayal of society, subculture, and even our state of being. Yes, you are your monster!

Vast schools of thought have posited theories to assist authors better. While I disagree with most of these assertions, it is worth mentioning one which authors might gain some benefit.

The *Compass Rose Model of Archetype Orientation* is a relatively new idea in Jungian-based literary philosophy. It posits archetypes have motivations which can be placed with other character archetypes along a compass rose. Instead of using cardinal directions, the model uses cardinal attributes, such as "Freedom," "Social," "Order," and "Ego" to name a few. Virtually any set of two opposed concepts, superimposed upon the other, can create an orientation, which drives a given archetype. For ego, a king will always represent "order" while a villain would be somewhere between "ego" and "freedom" using motivational directions on this compass rose example.

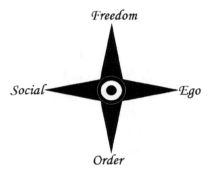

These tools help new writers to keep a clear understanding of what drives their character's archetype. More seasoned pen-men intuitively know these subconsciously driven desires.

Pay close attention to the allegory represented by a character type. A hero, a wizard, and a dwarf will always have the same motivation to save a damsel, find treasure, etc., in an odyssey plot. However, the message conveyed by each character will drastically change the story just by the allegory their archetype carries with it. No matter what the plotline suggests, archetypes will always provide great diversity to a story so long as a storyteller is true to their allegory. For example, the hero gets the girl and avenges the wronged, the wizard protects the innocent and uncovers hidden knowledge, and dwarves typically act with a duality where they state a baser reason for action while having an ulterior, and usu-ally altruistic, motivation they may not even be aware of – giving them a certain, unique nobility of character.

The following chapters are, therefore, intended to be vignettes into some of the most common archetypes used in literature, storytelling, and cinema. Mind you; this isn't meant to be an exhaustive work on the subject, but rather a quick resource for writers to use as a base reference point. Happy writing!

Chapter 1

Usage & Development

Archetypes, and their inherent allegory, provide writers with a unique psychological shorthand, which allows the story to be moved along without too much attention to character development. After all, a vampire is innately known by your audience already. Your job is merely to give direction, or *lanterns*, to the audience to let them know specific acknowledgments like, "this type of vampire can walk in the sun" or "this type of vampire can come back to life with a single drop of blood."

When using archetypal characters within a storyline, it is important also to provide context to further color/change deeply-entrenched allegory. Are you shifting the allegory any within the archetype? If so, you will need to be mindful of how this new archetypal allegory reacts compared to the traditional construct. Sometimes, archetypal regional characters may not be easily transferrable to all audiences. Therefore, it is critical to take into consideration your audience, your story's setting, and the innate nature of the archetypal character you are trying to use.

Generally speaking, most writers almost exclusively use humanoid archetypal characters. It is easier than dealing with the obtuse allegories attributed to non-humanoid archetypes – not that writers don't dabble as situations present themselves.

Non-Humanoid Character Usage

Non-humanoid archetypes speak to broad topics involving obtuse, even abstract, concepts. These constructs often include common concepts like power from sexual chastity, the burden/abuse of power, etc. We see this through carefully dissecting allegory from plots in stories based upon how a given archetype interacts with others.

A prime example of this is British-derived unicorn-based storylines where only the chaste can touch, and even kill, the mythical beast. The woman, still a virgin, has no lord and, therefore, is free and independent like the creature she pursues. At the climax of the story, the phallic horn and blood involved in these tales correlate to the woman losing her virginity. With her virginity being lost, she has transferred her power, and therefore her self-ownership, over to her lord.

The non-humanoid character is so unique and odd; it is sometimes challenging for most authors to utilize. For this reason, most non-humanoid archetypal characters are found only in science fiction and fantasy works.

For example, the *Lexx* television series (1997-2002) was rife with non-humanoid allegory as a mismatched crew escaped in an organic spaceship from a living planet – both the spaceship and planet being giant bugs. Here, these larger-than-life characters worked with humanoid archetypes to speak about humanity's inadequacies and how we are on an accelerated path to self-induced annihilation.

Conversely, Farscape (1999-2003) used non-humanoid archetypes, subtly, to speak to the human condition. The usage of leviathans, created by alien deities, is a fantastic play on the Apocryphal text found in 1 Enoch 60:7-8. In the show, Moya, a leviathan roaming the abyss of space, is defiled by the militaristic Peacekeepers to create a hybrid male behemoth named Talyn. The interplay of both Moya and Talyn created a unique back-drop in a fight of good against evil.

This obtuse allegory of non-humanoid archetypes is tricky and genre-limited. Unconventional usage has experimented within this class of archetypes because fans of the science fiction and fantasy genres are amenable to experimental character development. Rare texts and ancient mythology still today provide an excellent resource for character development. These have known storylines, with compelling characters, which can be manipulated to fit the era and locale of the work. Other sources can come from scientific journals and obscure works in the public domain.

Humanoid Character Usage

Humanoid archetypes are more discernable than non-humanoid archetypes and, therefore, address elements we can easily relate to and understand. In other words, humanoids represent us humans. The targeted audience already knows a king is always a leader, a villain is always a lawbreaker outside of civil society, etc.

In some plots, such as those found in science fiction and fantasy, fantastical humanoid creatures are used to relate more complex concepts such as puberty, homosexuality, racism, and more. With these creatures, as you will learn later in this book, even their very appearance and mannerisms help to resonate the intended allegory to the audience.

For this reason, it would make sense that most archetypal characters, used in literature and cinemas today, are humanoid. Writers can easily employ their allegory while readers readily understand hidden meanings the characters impart. Proper usage of archetypal characters and their associated allegories can be transformative to a story. However, the allegory of a character isn't always fixed. Indeed, an author can change our perceptions by playing upon our built-in biases.

In Stephanie Osborn's book, *El Vengador*, she masterfully wrote a werekin piece, which didn't use historical allegory tied to the specific archetype employed.

Typically, werewolf stories involve allusions to puberty, savage sexuality, physicality, etc. Werekin tales dealing with sasquatches, and others of similar ilk, generally have the same allegory tied to them, but with a less aggressive, almost environmentalist, and a somewhat humanitarian type of slant.

In Osborn's work, the creature alludes to cultural changes and long-held racial tensions/prejudices. She, therefore, creates a paradigm shift in a little changed historical archetype's symbolic representation.

S. R. Staley's award-winning book, *St. Nic, Inc.* took similar measures when addressing the social justice issues surrounding little people (a.k.a. dwarves).

In his work, Santa's *elves* were people of short stature who worked with the North Pole network to achieve economic prosperity and social equality not afforded to them in contemporary society. Here, the reader was forced to see an *elf* as a real person who, despite being highly capable and qualified, is generally overlooked and berated because of size alone.

Sometimes, change is not needed. For example, Zelle Andrews didn't change an archetype in her award-winning book,

Paisley Memories. Instead, she adeptly embraced a regional archetypal character to provide her book color, context, and balance.

Her character, *Butterball*, represents a specific type of Southern woman found mostly in North Florida. The archetype construct for this character involves a widowed, senior woman who is generally portly, friendly, earthy, hilariously uncouth, insightful, generous, somewhat blundering, and usually dependent upon family/friends while staunchly trying to maintain her independence. Such an archetypal character goes by an odd nickname like Butterball, Puddin, etc.

This type of character was fundamentally necessary to balance out Andrews' storyline involving the woes of a displaced, unwed, destitute, mother who lacked any family support for the care and raising of her Down Syndrome child. Andrews' primarily North Florida audience give high praise for the book because the majority knows a *Butterball* type of figure in their own personal lives.

Here, the author's playing upon shared experiences that equates into more involved readers who can put a specific face to Butterball. They can see their own Butterball doing much of what the character does in the book. For many, this character usually brings back fond memories of a past which can never be reclaimed. Therefore, while telling a story about a Down Syndrome child, the author is also providing an opportunity for readers to stroll through the memories of their childhood past.

Regional Character Development

Audiences grow tired of predictable archetypes. For almost thirty years, cinema treated vampires the same banausic, boring way. Most were either counts, or some other type of aristocrat, who bolted away from crosses, detested garlic, and was turned to dust by the light of the sun.

Today, vampires can walk out in the sun, eat garlic-laden pizzas, and even go to church! What changed?

Writers had to change the character to keep audiences interested. To do this, many used regional variations of vampire folklore to craft a new creature, which shifted both mannerism and allegory to fit contemporary needs and issues.

Regional variations of archetypal characters can be especially tricky. For instance, a *rougarou* is defined as a *lycanthrope* (a.k.a. *werewolf* or *werekin*) cryptid specific to many Louisiana communities.

Before the French took control of what we know today as Louisiana, the early Isleño culture of the Spanish-speaking Canary Islands pioneer immigrants told tales of a cryptid, which was far different than the Cajun beast. From a cultural perspective, Isleño swamp creature was more akin to the contemporary *chupacabra* than any oyster-shucking werewolf, or sasquatch, now portrayed as the rougarou.

Before the Isleños, various indigenous tribes had their own swamp monster archetypes, which bore little resemblance to either the Spanish or the French versions. This serves as a testament to how culture colors character portrayals and perceptions.

Imagine being a small play writer in Louisiana. Your *rougarou* character wouldn't even be called by that name in St. Bernard Parish because the locals speak a type of Pidgin Spanish. While the story is compelling, the allegory would be lost on many there. Once the play went on the road to other parishes, it'd run into other issues. For instance, the allegory could be especially lost on many in the Coushatta, Houma, and other tribes that have other names and cultural variations of the swamp monster. Then there are the Italians, Métis, and other prominent, but lesser known, cultures of this state, which may or may not relate at all with such a regional creature. Now, imagine these issues in each state! The astute writer should be wary of these, and neighboring sub-cultures of the same region, which may not appreciate nuanced cultural biases when regional archetypes are being used.

Another regional archetype variation is the Spanish *chupaca-bra* cryptid. Here, the creature varies substantially based upon culture and location.

For example, in the Caribbean, people describe the chupa-cabra as a large-eyed, almost reptilian, humanoid creature with spines, or quill-like projections along its back and tail. This dimin-utive creature, being only about the height of a grade school child, stands upon two legs and hops around like a kangaroo.

However, in Mexico and Texas, people describe the *chupa-cabra* as a gray, hairless, blue-eyed dog with a sometimes arched back and two fleshy lumps on its hindquarters.

Noticeably different from each other, both are said to kill animals only to drink their blood. Thus, writers must be excep-tionally fastidious in crafting a character to a specific audience.

Historical & Cultural
Character Development

History and cultural evolution can change the allegory and man-nerisms of an archetypal character. For instance, zombies are vastly different today than historical versions. Approximately 5,000 years ago, they were very similar to the Egyptian *mummy* or the subsequent Jewish *golem*. They carried allegories of reli-gious oppression for a plethora of reasons. From the 1960s to 1980s, the zombie archetype drastically morphed to represent enslavement. Today, the zombie character is akin to the listless, soullessly feeding ghouls of antiquity. Their allegory is now profoundly complex; speaking to humankind's naivety, cultural programming, and consumerism in a society, which doesn't have to hunt and forage for survival.

Other considerations can create dramatically varying traits in the portrayal of the character based on ethnicity and shared experiences. For instance, a Native American would have a different world view than an African American or Caucasian American. Race not considered, the experiences and sensibilities of a person hailing from rural Americana would contrast significantly with a metropolitan dweller. Thus, characters can change in a multitude of ways.

Staying True

Many storytellers fail because they use the wrong archetype to convey an allegory. Other times, the character is doing things which wouldn't be true to his/her past, current situation, or basic archetypal construct. The audience will eventually pick up on the various nuanced inconsistencies evident in the storyline. Naturally, the last thing any storyteller wants is for the audience to become disinterested!

Most times, archetype-rich characters can almost create a dynamic story themselves. A country-based creature will always favor wild "vittles" to the bland food of the city. A city dweller will always take umbrage at the lack of refinement, hard labor, and general dinginess of country life. Taking these considerations into play, a version of events can more easily play out. The more "over-the-top" an archetypal character is, the more it can move an otherwise depressing, or hopeless, plot along.

It's important to stay true to the mannerisms, motivations, and allegories of the character archetype in relation to your targeted audience. In *Paisley Memories*, Butterball would never do an expensive nightgown, board a jet to New York, and sip on champagne with cheese and caviar between waltzes. The readers would have immediately seen such as a blaring offense and revolted. Because the author stayed true to her audience and characters, she quickly became an award-winning author with glowing accolades and a follow-up book in the Paisley series.

Please note, this is not to say unintended audiences won't grumble now and then. Even in successes, like *Twilight*, Stephenie Meyer has been ridiculed by much of vampire fandom for her bedazzled depictions of the archetype. Vampire fans have also posted off-color memes online of things like Sesame Street's Count beating up Edward saying, "Vampires don't sparkle!" Despite the negative attention she has garnered, she is successful because of her laser-like focus on an ingénues-specific demographic. Had the books been marketed to the general vampire fandom, she would have been ousted as a "heretic" and "hack" rather than a best-selling author and recipient of multiple, lucrative movie contracts.

Timing

Sometimes, you can do everything right and still get it wrong. Oft times, books will have fantastic sales only to start a downward spiral to oblivion. Other times, you might see a movie turn out to be a box office flop just to have rentals skyrocket inexplicably. What is the missing variable in the equation for success? In regard to archetypes and allegory, the missing element tends to be timing.

Contrary to what Jung once taught, we now know audiences accept archetypes based on moments in their lives. Sometimes, it is their age that determines an affinity for a given archetype.

Other times, it might be a socio-economic, or socio-political, issues that draw audiences to a given archetype.

Think about it, after the 9/11 terrorist attacks, America was in a state of *shell shock*, or what we now call today *Post-Traumatic Stress Disorder (PTSD)*. We were sad, scared, humiliated, angry, and generally feeling all of the emotions a victim feels. So, how did the market respond? Superhero-themed songs, books, movies, etc., dominated popular culture. Later, once we began to understand the full scope of the *Arab Spring*, mummy-themed films and books began to soar. This is because the audience, based upon the conditions of the day, was primed to accept a given archetype. At first, we needed heroes to provide us with hope. Afterward, we utilized mummies, and their allegory representing a theological takeover of a culture, to understand how the enemy works.

For these reasons, young girls tend to favor stories of witches, werewolves, and brooding vampires. Meanwhile, young boys prefer hulking beasts, monster-slaying heroes, etc. This understanding is due to their age and hormonal changes, priming them to be receptive to given allegory represented by a given archetype.

We find this to be especially true in the 1990s when America was arresting more juveniles than all previous years of U.S. history combined. This war on youth, fueled primarily by performance-based education funding, in what experts now call the *School-to-Prison Pipeline*, eventually led to the rise of the comic book *anti-hero*.

Before the 1990s, most literary and cinematic heroic characters worked with law enforcement and the laws of society. However, when school resource officers began to flood schools, the iconic friendly police officer began to be perceived differently as students saw their peers being hauled off in handcuffs for innocuous offenses no adult would ever be arrested for (i.e., drawing a picture at school or using a French-fry as a toy gun). It became obvious to the youth that America's adults were against them. The anti-hero told the story of how good people can be deemed as evil, lawbreakers by many. It explained how a society becomes corrupt and how fighting the system might mean a decent and generally law-abiding person becomes vilified. It also suggested that bad choices do not necessarily mean one has to give up fighting for their soul and humanity.

Presidential administrations also have a similar impact on these changes in archetype acceptance. For example, between the middle of the George Walker Bush administration, and the end of the Barack Hussain Obama administration, we saw a rise in pirate allegory. The pirate represents a rebellion against a government, which does not fall in line with one's desire for personal freedoms. The Donald John Trump administration changed this uptick in pirate allegory. Soon, pirate-based book and movie sales began to decline. We also started to see a decline in vampire and werewolf stories as well while seeing an uptick in mermaid stories.

Please don't get me wrong; the rise or fall in allegory popularity has nothing to do with what these administrations physically did. Instead, much like the stock market, the rise and fall in demand are due precisely to emotions and perceptions the audience had towards the administrations.

So, what is the trick to selling a book or a screenplay rife with a given allegory? You guessed it, timing! For this reason, it may be wise for writers to consider stockpiling various stories for given societal events. This way, when a change takes place, one can dust off that old, archived manuscript and be the first to market for an eagerly awaiting audience.

Chapter 2

Non-Humanoid Archetypes

As stated earlier, there's a cavernous rift between the archetypes of humanoids and non-humanoids. Non-humanoid concepts are broader and less specific. In antiquity, non-humanoids represented elements of nature, purity, honesty, and other humanistic values missing in most societies. In a fashion, they were more of a force, or concept, rather than a specific trait.

Remember, the following characters are not an exhaustive list, but rather highlighted examples. Entire libraries exist on non-humanoid mythical beasts – more commonly referred to today as *cryptids*. As with all the archetypes listed in this book, always assume that for each archetype highlighted, there are at least twenty which are not.

Bear Dog

According to fossil evidence, there once was a creature called the bear dog which roamed the earth. It's the ancestor of both bears and dogs. A ferocious beast, the bear dog, has been the stuff of myths and legends in North America for several millennia. In Canada, it is sometimes called the *waheela* or *amaroq*. In Iowa, it's known as the *shunka warakin*. Meanwhile, in the Montana area, a hyena-like animal was killed and preserved by a taxidermist. This bear dog-type animal was called a *ringdocus*.

Being warm-blooded, the creature's archetypical allegory imparts intelligence, familiarity, and passionate violence we humans attribute to mammalian predators. It harkens back from a past in the collective unconscious we thought was long gone. It is from an era where everything was larger, more violent, and alien to our contemporary era.

In cinema and literature, its reason for being around is just as enigmatic as the reason why it may be stalking and killing people. Did we push it out of hiding? Is it nature's way of keeping humanity in check? Did a scientist go too far by unlocking something hidden in the DNA of our closest friend?

Whatever the reason, these animals are very ancient. They have instincts we can't even comprehend. And yet, their appearance is new, exciting, and frightening because they shouldn't exist.

As familiar to us as our fearless friend, the dog, we innately know in our bones that these creatures are in the wrong timeline. This creature is an enigma and a conflict between new and old in the hunt not only for the beast, but also finding what brought it to our time.

Acari

The *acari electricus*, sometimes called *acari crossi* after Andrew Crosse, is a tick-like mite found to be growing in a hostile environment of various chemicals subjected to an electrical current. Michael Faraday, a noted scientist, replicated Crosse's work. However, as Crosse's research became lost to time, people doubted the existence of such a creature.

An interesting historical fact is, after discovering the acari, Crosse met Mary Shelley, the author of *Frankenstein; or, The Modern*

Prometheus. Ironically, Frankenstein's monster and Crosse's acari bore a very similar genesis story.

Over the years, this chance meeting of two iconic figures has not been lost on the storytellers. For instance, in the 2001 film, *Jason X*, writers used ant-like robots to create a super-monster. Elsewhere, television shows, like *Stargate SG-1* (1997-2007), *Stargate: Atlantis* (2004-2009), and *Doctor Who* (1963-Present), all have depicted mite-like, self-replicating robots not only destroying entire worlds, but also evolving at an exponential rate.

In acari-based archetypes, it is very much like the bear dog in the fact that it shouldn't exist. However, there is an organic, also alien, nature which we both identify with and are yet put off by its very being. Typically represented as a creature of technology, it uses our tools against us either by creating monsters, rendering our weapons useless, or by turning our machines against us somehow.

There is something sacred to the acari as well because they are often a "new" lifeform deserving of preservation and understanding. Sadly, humans have always failed to recognize the rights of other lifeforms. This motivates the developing acari to fight back and swarm humanity in a takeover.

In more recent manifestations, the allegory of this archetype would imply it wanted to be like humans – seeing us not as enemies, but somewhat as older siblings to emulate and one day surpass. Sometimes, this even means taking on human form.

In rare instances, the acari are representative of unity. Often perceived as a dark force, it can also be surprisingly benevolent. For example, in the 2018 movie, *The Nutcracker and the Four Realms, the rat king* archetype was played out in the historical fashion of an acari creature. First portrayed as malevolent, and then benevolent, the creature is nothing more than a multitude of rats working in concert with each other much like fish do in a school – only with a weird sentience trait to the creature. Similar usage of the acari archetype also played out in the 2018 movie, *Ralph Breaks the Internet*. Both are Disney films.

Increasingly, the acari archetype is becoming more complex and less mechanized. For example, *Star Trek: Discovery* (2017-Present) depicts a multidimensional *mycelial network* (fungal network), which is sentient and can replicate humanoid form.

Somewhat similar, it could be said, whether intentional or not, that the *Andromeda* (2000-2005) television series used the acari archetype to explore Luke 19:39,40 of the *Holy Bible*. In this passage, after being harassed by the Pharisees to rebuke His followers, Jesus tells them the rocks along the road would cry out if the people kept quiet over His presence. Did this passage infer that rocks had a soul and are sentient? Did Jesus verify a previously popular pagan concept that nature is self-aware?

In this vein, Trance Gemini (portrayed by Laura Bertram) proved to be a marvelous experiment in acari archetype development. Here, Trance starts as an insignificant, but mysterious, figure which is later revealed to be an avatar for a furious star wishing to go back to her home solar system after being cast out by an ancient, and presumed extinct, race of alien beings.

The allegory was fantastic as multiple dimensional avatars of the star could communicate with each other, replace each other in a given timeline, etc. This opened a host of questions, which will inevitably color future writers' works. For instance, "How would something as old and powerful as a sentient star react to corporeal beings?" Better yet, Trance Gemini's character further colors things by showing how the acari archetype can remain socially camouflaged for years without ever revealing any significant elements of a much larger, and premeditated, plot.

Trance proved that the acari archetype can use our own diversity, egos, and self-serving agendas to its favor in order to hide, and even guide, others along a chosen path without anyone being the wiser for it.

Unicorns

As stated in an earlier chapter, unicorns have a virgin-specific allegory attributed to them. For this reason, they are more popular with children's stories than young adult or adult pieces.

The contemporary version of a unicorn is a horse with a single, spiraled horn jutting from the head – called an alicorn. Sometimes, it is even morphed with the pegasus archetype by adding wings to it – thus conflating the two allegories into one.

In the *Holy Bible*, various translations of texts speak of a unicorn. We find it mentioned in Job 39:9-12, Deuteronomy 33:17, Numbers 23:33, Numbers 24:8, Psalms 22:21, and Psalms 92:10. Scholars suggest some translations mistook the re'em, a species of gigantic, possibly mythological/extinct, half-domesticated, wild oxen as being the unicorn of antiquity. This gave the unicorn a holy connotation from the Medieval through the Neo-Classical periods. While not specifically mentioned in the Bible, Christian folklore and song tells of Noah not being able to get the unicorns to board the ark. Some even accuse Noah's son for this blunder.

Initially, the unicorn was depicted as a beast which was a part horse, part goat, having a stag-like head, shaggy feet, cloven hooves, and the trademark singular spiraling horn on the forehead. The Greeks treated the animal as real, rather than mythical, and living primarily in India.

Later, Europeans fashioned fantastical unicorn-based stories. One said the Virgin Mary was able to tame the beast and make it fall asleep. This led to a wide-held belief a virgin could only tame the unicorn. Once asleep, it would be slain, and its horn severed from the body for alchemy purposes.

The horn was believed to heal and to purify water. Traders often sold male narwhal tusks as unicorn horns for religious artwork. One such item, the famous Thrown Chair of Denmark, is said to be made of unicorn horns – now known to be narwhal tusks. Cups were also sold to monarchs since they were always under the fear of being poisoned and legend had it that unicorn horns could destroy poisons.

While a rarity in most adult literature, the allegory of unicorns is mostly fixed, thanks to the Medieval Era European Christians. This beast represents power and purity tied to a woman's virginity. No longer a virgin, she'd become chattel to her mate.

For this reason, the market is now set for experimental storytellers to craft a new allegory for this character – something which must be done if this character is ever to gain any popularity in the adult literary market. A brief example of such a deviation is found with the television series, *DC's Legends of Tomorrow* (2016-Present), where the unicorn's portrayed as a flesh-eating, demonic beast, which is drawn to sexual energy and uses a psychedelic drug as a defense mechanism. In this interpretation, the unicorn was an allegory for the pitfalls of the somewhat naïve, and free-willed, 1960s era.

Pegasus

Technically, the name for a specific mythological animal, all winged horses, are now called a *pegasus* individually and *pegasi* in the plural form. While never technically an immortal in original folklore, this creature is today considered timeless, benevolent, and honorable.

In the mythic history of the character, it was the heroic steed of the Muses. It was said to be the delayed offspring from Poseidon's raping of Medusa – the beast only springing forth once Medusa's head was severed. Not knowing the pedigree of this beast, storytellers often invent tales of their own. These stories generally impart an allegory representing divine favor and providence.

To invoke a pegasus into a storyline is to say the hero is highly favored by divine forces and is beyond reproach. If it is a *unicorn pegasus*, sometimes referred to as an *alicorn* in contemporary writings, one will typically find a heroine almost always riding it. Here, she is most likely a virgin without peer or lord to tame her. During the 1980s, the *She-Ra* cartoons used such a character for the heroine's steed and with her only peer being her twin brother, *He-Man*.

Chimera

Conflict is said to be the universal plot. Conflict is also the creator of archetypes. With cultural conflicts, between Asia Minor and Mediterranean Europe, the chimera embodied the allegories surrounding the two drastically different cultures.

The Chimera was originally depicted as the child of two horrible gods, Typhon and Echidna. Among its many siblings were the dreaded Hydra and Cerberus. This creature breathed fire and had a lion's body and head, a goat's head along its back (facing backward), and a serpent's head at the end of its tail.

Later, Asian influences adapted the character to also have wings. The Hittites changed out the backward-facing goat head for a forward-facing human one. Still, others adopted the creature even more.

Today, a chimera is defined as a singular, transgenic animal having the DNA of two, or more, genetically different animal species. For instance, scientists routinely make real-life chimeras out of lab rats, fish, and others by adding bioluminescent jellyfish DNA – the result being animals which glow in the dark. Other animals are made into chimeras using the DNA of drastically different creatures for a multitude of purposes. One example is the growing usage of transgenic goats, which have spider DNA in them. Scientists hope to create a cheap, biodegradable, bio-polymer, which is narrower, and stronger, than either Kevlar® or steel. The goats may look like an ordinary goat, but their milk has spider's web material which has to be filtered out and specially spun to create the biopolymer.

While some adult-centered works vaguely speak of trans-genic creatures, most chimera depictions that are found in Asian, and Middle Eastern, inspired works mostly geared to young children.

The allegory of these creatures can be diverse, but it is all birthed from conflict and fear. Middle Eastern terrorism, Asian market takeover of America, natural law abuses made by scien-tists, etc., all use the chimera as both a highlighting of the con-flict and also as a warning should things get out of hand.

Dragons

Nothing quite depicts human frailty like having a dragon staring you down. Virtually every culture has its version of these chi-mera-like serpent cryptids. Despite entire cultures, separated by multiple millennia of seclusion from other cultures, most claim dragons to be real even though scientists say they never existed.

According to world cultures, these creatures all look different and yet they have similar attributes. Most enjoy the water, can fly, have mystical powers, sport horns or antlers on their heads, and usually breathe fire. And, except for the Maori, and a few other historical/cultural depictions, all dragons are snake-like. Later, in Medieval Europe, the creature grew legs, a lion-like torso, and even a pot belly in some cases.

Even in the New World, various tribes all have their flying, mostly horned, and usually iridescent "feathered serpents." For the Aztec, his name is *Quetzalcoatl*. Before them, the Mayans had *Q'uq'umatz*. With the Cherokee, his name is *Uktena*. For the Creeks, he is *Estakwvnayv*. The Choctaw spoke of their *Sinti Lapitta*. The Albaamaha (a.k.a. Alabama Tribe, the namesake of the State of Alabama) call theirs *Tcinto Såktco*. For many Pueblo tribes, his name's revered as *Avanyu*. And, the Sioux call their dragon *Uncegila*.

Dragons, by nature, are generally capricious. Creatures of the abstract, they exist between the borders of our reality and somewhere beyond our comprehension. Until Christianity came along, a sort of holiness had been associated with dragons. Only the purest and noblest could even meet with a dragon and live. Some cultures believed in a duality, based upon perception and purity, between *angel* and *dragon*. Later, the dragon exclusively became associated with Lucifer.

Today, dragons can impart a wide swath of moldable allegory. In Christian fiction pieces, it can depict evil. In neo-Pagan works, it can represent divine enlightenment. Secular works can use it to represent nature out of balance, as with the *Godzilla* movie franchise. When transformed into a human form, dragons are being used to impart how homosexual and bisexual mannerisms are inherent to nature.

It's the easiest of all non-humanoid characters to use in a story because the dragon is one of the few universal archetypes known to most of humanity. Even more so than the bear dog, it is ancient and innately "known" to the audience. Therefore, some reverence for the archetype still needs to be adhered to — however abstract it may be.

Thunderbirds

While far less common than dragons, several cultures talk about huge birds able to carry off livestock and even humans. Ironically, unlike the dragon, some evidence can be found of these birds once existing in real life.

The Haast's eagle, considered by academics to be the same as the *Pouakai* (South Island) and *Hokioi* (North Island) of Maori legend, was the second-largest eagle to have ever lived. Its prey, the moa, was a flightless fowl weighing almost 500 pounds. Ironically, some scientists posit the Haast's eagle died out around the 1300s to 1400s only because the Maori had hunted the moa to extinction. This might explain why the Maori had numerous tales of giant birds attacking children and even adults.

The only eagle larger than the Haast's was North America's Woodward's eagle. Woodward's eagle covered the majority of the New World — including the Caribbean. Probably the inspiration for *thunderbirds*, these creatures would have been able to carry off small children with ease.

Despite enormous distances from each other, stories of the Cherokee's *Tlanuwah* and the Maori's *Hokioi/Pouakai* have many similarities regarding the creatures preying on humans, having black and red colorations, etc. Cherokee warriors even wore red and black in honor/memory of the tlanuwah. Other tribes naturally have similar stories.

In almost all cases, these birds control the sky while the dragons control the water. Sometimes, the two were said to have engaged in horrific battles with each other. Usually, it was the thunderbird who'd win by snatching the dragon up out of the water and dispatching it with its sharp beak.

These birds were capricious entities. Feared by humankind, their tales also talk about how humanity caused them to leave – often negatively changing the forces of nature. Possibly, for this reason, these creatures are said only to show themselves at a time of great injustice. When seen in a vision, the person is believed to have been divinely picked out as a grand champion of the people.

Such allegory is not lost on literature and cinema. J.R.R. Tolkien's *Lord of the Rings* series of books speaks explicitly of great eagles flying off the heroes on their backs. In children's stories, giant eagles again are said to be guardians and keepers of the peace.

Sea Monsters, Leviathans & Behemoths; Oh My!

Humanity is intrigued by large, powerful creatures. Sometimes, they can be of use to us. In most cases, they end up killing us. They are immovable elements to put into check man's unstoppable thirst for more. The resulting fallout is almost always of epic proportions.

Most sea monsters are allegories for humanity putting nature out of balance in ways both unseen and unfelt. In the movie franchise, *Jaws*, great white sharks attacked people assumedly because humanity had changed its environment so much it now saw people as prey. In the 1977 film, *Orca*, a large marine animal hunter kills a bull orca's mate and then casts her dead fetus overboard in sight of the male – which later exacted his revenge. Before these, *Kraken* were said to attack sailing ships – presumably because humanity was exceeding his rightful domain by trying to tame the seas.

Since the story of Jonah, *leviathans* have always been carriers of wayward champions and the roamers of lonely oceans. More akin to earlier versions of dragons than today's whales, these creatures were also exacters of God's revenge in early Hebrew theology – as evidenced in Job 40. On land, especially in the desert areas, is the *behemoth*. This creature, also referenced in Job 40, is also an exacter of God's revenge – meaning humanity was neither safe from His judgment on land or sea.

While the leviathans and the behemoths roam sea and land equally, in both literary and cinematic works, contemporary archetypes for these characters have changed little. Sometimes, the two are conflated while at other times separate.

As for sea creatures, their allegory has also changed little. It is always nature putting humanity in check for wrongful behaviors/actions. The movie, *Deep Blue Sea* (1999), showed what happens when transgenic human/shark hybrids are misused to fight Alzheimer's Disease. A sequel, done in 2018, had a similar storyline. Meanwhile, cinematic stories like *Loch Ness* (1996) and *The Water Horse* (2007) show there are things still unknown about our world and which need protection at all costs.

CHAPTER 3

Sci-Fi/Fantasy Humanoid Archetypes

Witches, wendigos, krampuses, werewolves, fairies/elves, vampires, aliens, zombies, mermaids, and mummies – these creatures make up the bulk of science fiction and fantasy archetypes. Each one has a history and allegory unique unto itself.

Because this chapter deals with archetypal characters better known to humanity's collective unconsciousness, their descriptions and background will be brief. Lesser utilized characters will not be covered in this chapter. Therefore, you are urged to consult other references when necessary.

Witches & Warlocks

The allegory behind *witches* has changed little in both literature and cinema. This doesn't mean they are all portrayed the same. For instance, L. Frank Baum's *The Wonderful Wizard of Oz* depicts a drastically different witch than the ones found in L. J. Smith's novel series, *The Vampire Diaries*.

The *witch* archetype is feminine-based much like the unicorn's character is. While she once represented an agent and concubine of the *Devil*, she's now a symbol of female empowerment.

To balance out this empowerment, most storytellers wish to include a powerful *warlock* to act as a male antagonist. Lacking morals, and desiring to unbalance nature, the warlock represents contemporary society's hatred of dominant male behavior. Sometimes, this is more subtly played out by making the warlock either homosexual or bisexual, as is done in Cassandra Clare's own, The *Shadowhunter Chronicles.* Even here, warlocks are made to be the offspring of demons and not angels.

For these reasons, witches are generally found in *chic-lit* and *chic-flic* genres (both are terms I loathe for their sexist connotations). Here, the witch only concerns herself with issues and viewpoints usually only identifiable, and resonating with, women. In young adult pieces, the witch is generally soft-spoken, possibly introverted, and emotionally or physically troubled. Her witchcraft becomes her voice and a source of female empowerment. Missing from these ingénue-biased works are strong, positive warlocks.

Warlocks are better suited to an older audience in stories where the witch is mature, been through a lot, and the warlock represents a reminder of male oppression of the female identity. With growing rarity, the warlock figure is replaced with the historic *Devil* figure.

Because of our society's latent, negative bias towards a strong male identity; the warlock is rarely depicted as a positive figure in cinematic, or literary, works. If such a figure is presented positively, he is almost always called a *wizard, magician,* or *mage* and not a practitioner of earth-based magic.

Werekin

In Native American cultures, the *Wendigo* is the epitome of evil. For many, this creature is as close to the *Devil* as one can come. Being a sort of cannibalistic, weredeer demon, it has the unique ability to shapeshift. Its allegory is associated with mental/emotional health issues going undiagnosed and untreated for too long. Today's works now are increasingly using wendigo characters to represent little talked about issues like PTSD in war veterans. The latter was seen in the television show, *Sleepy Hollow* (2013-2017).

The *Krampus* is a *werekin* of a different category. A *weregoat* type of *demon*, its kind are slaves to *Santa Claus* in many Germanic legends. Sometimes managed by a keeper, named *Black Peter* or *Zwarte Piet*, Santa Claus sends them to deal with naughty children. This can mean enslavement, drowning, or outright cannibalism by the monsters. They represent Christian conflict as well as family discord, youthful defiance, and child abuse/neglect. While not well known in America, some works, like the movie *Krampus* (2015), and *Krampus: The Devil Returns* (2016), have received positive viewer praise. For information about this Christmas monster and more, please consult my forthcoming book, *A. Scrooge's Christmas Compendium*.

Werewolves are a historical archetype with firm roots in France. At one time, werewolf trials were as commonplace in France as witchcraft trials were in colonial America and Great Britain. They usually involved a witch acting as an agent of the Devil to entrap a man into a contract for his soul. This person was then killed as an unwilling slave to *Lucifer*. Therefore, witches are often paired in werewolf-based plotlines even if the Devil is omitted from contemporary, secular storylines.

Werewolf allegory once represented nature being off-kilter because of the evilness of humankind. Today, they represent raw sexuality, dominant masculinity, male teen pubescence, and repressed urges creating a duality in one's persona. This is why the Comic Code Authority once forbade the usage of werewolves, the words "wolf man," or any other such sources of *werekin* allegory which would play into the hormonal urges of juvenile males going through puberty. The CCA's fear of this allegory was so strong; DC Comics' Marv Wolfman couldn't get his stories approved because of his last name!

Naturally, other parts of the world have various werewolf tales. Some werewolves aren't even wolves at all! For this reason, the term *werekin* has been coined to refer to any man/creature humanoid. Of course, not all werekin must be animals. Robert Louis Stevenson's *The Strange Case of Dr. Jekyll and Mr. Hyde* proves this point by playing up the duality of persona caused by repression. Later, when comics couldn't use werewolf themes, the atypical werekin story of *Jekyll and Hyde* was used to create Marvel's *The Incredible Hulk* comic book. With the success of the *Hulk*, other characters were created. This translated into both television series and movies. Subsequently, when CCA rules relaxed, traditional werewolf/werekin characters were brought into comic plotlines. By then, entire generations grew up on puberty and repressed rife allegories played up in the Hulk-based comics, television shows, and movies.

Contemporary books and television shows, like *Lost Girl* (2010-2015) and *Grimm* (2011-2017), use a host of werekin characters. Each one has its specific allegory tied to it, making the archetype more diverse and less prominent as a standalone character in a story arc.

Sirens

Several creatures can represent a sexual allegory. Each archetypal character colors the allegory differently. *Mermaids* (a.k.a. *sirens*) are an extension of the classic *femme fatale* allegory. Beautifully seductive, with alluring song, they led men to their deaths in ancient lore.

Lately, another type of allegory has arisen. These works play off an alternate evolutionary path where humanity's early ancestors were trapped and, therefore, had to return to the seas. Depicted more like a weredolphin or were-whale, these sirens are the victims of humankind's intrusion into the ocean. Their allegory is laden with environmental overtones and significant jabs at the military for damaging marine life.

In contemporary culture, the mermaid is a figure that speaks to female frailty and deep emotion. One could say its allegory is tainted by children's books and movies. For example, Hans Christian Andersen's *The Little Mermaid* tells the story of a mermaid who must suffer pain, much akin to walking on razor blades, to be with her beloved only for him to find love in the arms of another woman. This causes the mermaid to commit suicide. Only the purity of her love saves her as she becomes one of the Daughters of the Air to do good deeds for 300 years in hopes of one day attaining a soul. This is a drastically different story than what we see in today's children's books and movies, like Disney's *The Little Mermaid*.

Ironically, while the mermaid in Andersen's story is known to be a strictly female archetype, it is theorized by historians to be an allegory for a homosexual relationship Andersen possibly had. However, historians disagree as to whether the relationship was sexual or merely the case of a strong, heterosexual friendship being misinterpreted through conventional lenses.

Much like the witch, the mermaid today speaks of female empowerment. Again, it is deeply hidden emotions and connection with nature that makes these creatures become special. Though not as prominent as witch stories, one can still see them in television series like *Siren* (2018-Present).

Nosferatu

The dead live and walk among us, stealing our maidens and drinking their blood – this is the story of the *nosferatu* (a.k.a. *vampire*). Like other science fiction and fantasy characters, vampires can naturally address issues of sexual innuendo. Contemporary vampires are the epitome of allegories involving congress and climax. Naturally, this trend started with Bram Stoker's *Dracula* and has continued to this day.

Apart from sexual lust, the vampire can represent a host of other allegories. Usually part of a cabal, vampires can be a way to represent secret government operations, corporate corruption, etc. The *Underworld* movie franchise is a prime example of this allegory.

Vampires have become a fantastic way to use multiple allegories. If you need to represent racism without being obvious – merely create a sub-class of vampires considered to be inferior and former slaves to the master race of vampires. Vampires can be gay or homeless or even suffering from HIV/AIDS-like diseases. Charlaine Harris proved this to be true in her *The Southern Vampire Mysteries* series of novels, which became HBO's hit show, *True Blood*.

This archetype has surely represented just about every form of allegory that storytellers have been able to imagine!

Mummies

Sparingly used in adult literary and cinematic works, *mummies* have increasingly been used in juvenile fiction books. This is because of the fact that they often tie-in with classroom teaching materials. Therefore, allegory is not a primary consideration in these stories.

With adult works, the *mummy* is almost always an allegorical reference to regime changes embroiled in religious overtones. *The Mummy Returns* movie of 2001 is a prime example.

Released in May, it was doomed to be a flop. After September 11, 2001, interest in the film grew. Why? Islamic terrorists had just attacked America. As anti-Islamic sentiment increased, so did the popularity of the movie. Hence, the power of a well-defined allegory was tied to a specific archetype!

Once Americans grew tired of the Islamophobia rhetoric, sales declined. Later, movie executives made a horrific blunder by trying to tie mummy allegory to American fears of Chinese dominance. *The Mummy: Tomb of the Dragon Emperor*, came out in 2008 and quickly was ridiculed as a symptom of the franchise being past its prime. Indeed, it was most likely a case of writers not paying enough attention to entrenched allegory within an archetype. The fourth movie in the franchise abruptly was canceled.

Aliens

A few years back, I was fortunate enough to get an interview with the movie writer and producer, Kenneth Johnson. Having the same first and last name didn't hurt either! Growing up, he was "Mr. Sci-Fi" to me. So, getting to pick his brain was a rare treat.

Honestly, I was somewhat shocked listening to him speak about his 1980s television series, V. While he flatly denied archetypal characters serving as an allegory in his works, he ironically mentioned how V was originally a story about fascism until television executives urged him to make the characters into *aliens*. According to the executive, it would be easier for audiences to accept the fascists as aliens than as humans. So, at least for the television executives, they acknowledged the power of archetypes and allegory even if an iconic screenwriter, and professor on the subject, could/would not.

Aliens are a unique type of archetype because their allegory allows them to represent any cultural conflict easily.

In *Star Trek: Deep Space Nine* (1993-1999), many of the episodes were practically rife with racism and social justice allegories. Once, there even was a baseball scene where all the alien players, of a competing team, had to be tagged because they all looked the same. Let's be honest here; very few archetypes would allow a writer to infuse such racist allegory into a storyline. And, the truth is, you can use practically any element of society with similar ease!

For this reason, the BBC's *Doctor Who* television series (1963-Present) perpetually produces episodes dealing with homosexuality and issues of bestiality. Really, how can you deny bestiality when the half cat people are marrying humans and having litters of kittens!

However bold *Doctor Who* may seem to critics, its spinoff series, *Torchwood* (2006-2011), is even more brazen, and over-the-top, with the sexually-charged, bisexual Capt. Jack Harkness (portrayed by John Barrowman, MBE) tackling alien dangers while freely having sex with anyone and everyone he can get his hands on – usually a man. One of the villains was even Capt.

Jack's lover (portrayed by James Marsters) whose kiss packed a potent knockout punch.

The look of the alien can also tell a lot about the allegory it is trying to convey. For instance, the *Klingons* of the *Star Trek* franchise (1966-Present), and *Moclans* of *The Orville* (2017-Present), noticeably portray all the biases that contemporary society has against males.

Big, less intelligent, somewhat feral, sexually charged, duty-driven, and hideously formed – there can be little doubt what allegory these fictional races impart. Seldom is a feminine race ever depicted in such a way!

Instead, aliens representing feminine elements tend to be beautiful, enlightened, strong, and capable. The Xelayans, of the *Orville*, is such an exemplar of this character type.

Indeed, in the world of storytelling, the alien archetype is the general panacea to imbue plotlines with cultural conflict allegories. Even better than a vampire, it can represent anything and everything. How the aliens treat humankind further colors the allegory in the minds of the audience.

Otherkins

Some storytellers have combined a litany of characters into a broad category to convey a host of allegories. These are referred to as *otherkins*. In the television series, *Lost Girl*, the otherkins were called *fae*. Conversely, Terry Brooks, in his *Shannara* novels, calls them *the four races*. However, some writers are more deliberate in naming the characters for what they are. For example, Nina Berry directly calls the characters *otherkins* in her series of novels aptly titled *Otherkin*.

Fairies, *elves*, *sprites*, and other such creatures can mean different things for different age groups. Therefore, one must use extra caution when working with otherkin archetypes. Also, because they are lumped together, the writer must know of cultural allegories within the audience.

For instance, the Cherokee, the Irish, and the Maori all have stories involving *leprechaun*-like beings. So, you never know how someone may perceive a character. Therefore, focus on how each character acts and reacts along a specific story arc.

Plant-based humanoids are considered to be kind, wise, helpful, playful, spiritual/contemplative, and even inventive.

Insectoids are considered the coldest, most amoral, and darkest of otherkin – making for great plot twists when an author, or scriptwriter, initially makes them out to be the good guys in a story.

Reptiles represent a similar allegory as insectoids but with a little more commonality for the audience. Still, they generally cannot be trusted.

Aquatic otherkin are unknown, mysterious, powerful, extremely slow or fast, cunning, and prone to ambush an opponent. If portrayed as an aquatic mammalian, one can often see that allegories include benevolence, powerfulness, a calculating mind, and remarkable resourcefulness.

Avian otherkin are free, sometimes dim-witted, spiritual, daring, powerful, graceful, and somewhat like aquatics in both aspects of speed and their propensity to ambush opponents. Because of American milliner history, some avian otherkin represent extinct, or rare creatures who were hunted nearly to extinction.

Mammalian otherkin are considered dark, passionate, vicious, cunning, and relentless. These otherkin use trickery and subterfuge with ease. The closer the otherkins are to humans, the more they are perceived to be like us and, therefore, less alien.

Some otherkin types are deemed as higher, or older, classes. For instance, there are the elemental types which embrace the forces of nature. These elemental otherkin are portrayed as exceptionally old, capricious, somewhat primal, adhering to a specific set of unspoken rules, and lacking any care for humanity.

In contrast, spiritual or multi-phasic otherkin are creatures of the ether able to touch without fear of being affected by others. They have their own set of rules where humankind is deemed to be out of place or wrongly elevated in an unstated hierarchy of evolution. At best, they hold a grudge against humanity. At worst, they want us to become extinct.

Terrestrial beings are a mix of old and higher classes of otherkin. These are creatures from the Earth itself (i.e., gnomes, sprites, elves, and fairies). Often unseen, they are the keepers of secrets. Humankind is something they know well and, therefore, try to avoid. Why they hide from us is their secret to keep. Obviously, humankind has injured them in the past, and they see little change in our baser nature. Only the select few can even view them. Even then, first encounters can end up being traumatic and even deadly.

Zombies, Golems & Ghouls

Zombies were once like *mummies* in their allegory. They also used to share allegory with Jewish *golems*. For centuries, they occupied a specific niche of allegory as an archetypal character. In a way, Mary Shelley's novel, *Frankenstein; or, The Modern Prometheus,* used a zombie-like golem for Adam (a.k.a., Frankenstein's Monster).

Unlike mummies of the era, which alluded to control and rule, the zombies and golems of Shelley's day represented breaking away from control. Like man's falling-away from God, these monsters always revolted against their creators. Thus, they represent a specific hubris in humankind.

Starting around the late 1960s, and ending around the late 1980s, zombies broke away from golems to morph their allegoric connotations. Here, these newly evolved archetypes portrayed wayward souls trapped by fear and superstition. Still carrying religious overtones in their allegory, they represented people with weak minds and wills conned by religious persons of authority. They also represented slavery in various aspects ranging from actual human slavery to addiction. The latter was especially true when ingredients, like datura stramonium (a.k.a., Jimson Weed or Zombie Cucumber), are (mis)used.

Later, in the 1990s, the zombie merged with the *ghoul*. Until then, the ghoul was a mindless, soulless creature feeding on the living and dead alike. The ghastly ghoul represented a very specialized type of allegory, which the 1990s era zombies quickly assumed.

Today, television shows, like *The Walking Dead* (2010-Present), represent a dystopic, consumeristic society of mindless souls lacking any power of control. Anyone having any original thought or actions is mercilessly attacked until they conform.

Zombies create a unique opportunity for storytellers using this archetype. Does it get faster or slower with age? Can it become human again? These questions, and more, further color the allegory.

Meanwhile, where a social revolt is needed, the zombie is no longer an appropriate archetype to use considering its conflation with the ghoul. Therefore, a golem is more commonly used – especially if it is revolting against humanity.

Lately, writers have depicted the golem as a flawed protector. In this vein, the crafty storyteller can use the golem to represent abusive step-parents, etc., in a child's life.

In some Japanese manga, and anime-based works, like the *Fullmetal Alchemist* franchise (2001-2017), the golem represents a horrific wrong one who is trying to make right – even if it can never be reversed. In this case, Edward Eric turns the lost soul of his little brother, Alphonse, into a specific type of golem – an empty suit of armor with a blood seal binding. The two then work to further this wrong against nature by attempting ways to bring Alphonse totally back to life as a living, breathing, human boy.

Homunculi

A *homunculus* is a remnant of archaic thought humanity once held about biology called preformationism. The concept rejects the notion of life coming together from bits and pieces and instead asserts that life comes preformed. Therefore, the act of propagation was believed to merely place this perfectly formed person (lying dormant in the sperm) into a perfect vessel (the egg) so that it might mature into a person. When it was an animal, this microscopic being was called an *animalcule*.

With alchemy giving way to science, we now no longer use preformationism as a valid understanding of how life replicates. However, this does not mean we do not still use homunculi in literary, televised, and cinematic storylines. Animalcules, on the other hand, seldom are referenced in literary and cinematic works – meaning there is an opportunity to create a new allegory.

Historically, the homunculi archetype has been used as an allegory to reference minorities and the oppressed. Practically any small group, or group without a voice, can be represented by this archetype.

In some cases, it is used to discuss the transitioning of the soul. For example, Mary Shelley's *Frankenstein; or, The Modern*

Prometheus is believed by many literary historians to be the retelling of Johann Conrad Dippel's desire to take a homunculus soul and create a man. On the opposite end of the spectrum, *Faust: The Second Part of the Tragedy*, by playwright Johann Wolfgang von Goethe, captures where the finest and brightest elevation of the human soul is when it leaves the body and passed on to the spiritual plane.

Space operas, such as the *Star Trek* franchise, the *Earth: Final Conflict* television series (1997-2002), the *Star Gate* franchise, and the *Babylon 5* television series (1994-1998) have all experimented with the Faustian concept of the spiritual homunculus. Oft times, in space operas, this spiritual elevation is an allegory for scientific reasoning vs. religion. While the writers may contend that both can elevate the souls of some, religion is portrayed as a trap for the souls of the majority while advancing only a select few. Science, on the other hand, is portrayed as elevating anyone who wishes to partake. Thus, the writers are making science to be a religion unto itself.

Regarding the argument that one can place a soul into a vessel, as a culturalist, I reject this as a homunculus archetypal concept. I contend that Frankenstein's monster was a golem. The golem archetype, though admittedly not called a golem until later in Jewish history, predates the homunculi by well over two thousand years. It is my sole contention that literary historians have conflated these two archetypal concepts. For this reason, I am also hesitant to accept the Faustian concept as being homunculi fully. Instead, I have only included it in this book for the reader's edification and academic reflection.

Instead, I tend to favor homunculi as being archetypes for thoughts and concepts relating to the disparaged, minority groups, etc. The *Fullmetal Alchemist* franchise, of manga and anime, shows what happens when humanity goes against God by turning these wayward souls into demented homunculi. The *Wreck-It Ralph* movies (2012, 2018) use homunculi, in a cyber world, to serve as a life allegory for young children. And, in numerous films and television shows, homunculi have been depicted as thoughts and persons living inside of the human mind.

Ironically, despite massive claims of racism and social injustice in contemporary society, authors and screenwriters today do not use homunculi to represent these stories. This is an important occurrence to note and may indicate there is significant room for writers to explore. The only caveat to this notion is that homunculi tend to flourish in cultures which believe in an afterlife. With a large part of American culture rejecting the thoughts of an afterlife, it might be wise to adopt the homunculus into something that is new and walks a thin line between being a concept and being a spirit. Still, it is a very achievable endeavor worth pursuing.

CHAPTER 4

Human Archetypes

Loch Ness-type monsters and werewolves are nice, but these aren't the only archetypes existing in literature and cinema. Most archetypal characters portrayed in stories are segments of society. The *teacher*, the *healer*, the *hero* — these are the common elements we are most familiar with in contemporary fiction.

This chapter briefly covers the most common archetypal characters and the allegory they represent. Naturally, as with the bulk of this book, this is merely a small listing of many archetypal characters which exist in literature and cinema. Please consult with other resources on the matter for less frequently used, or regional, character types.

Heroes/Anti-Heroes

A *hero* is generally someone who is compelled, often with a moral sense of duty, to run towards danger rather than from it. The hero typifies all that is good and virtuous in humanity.

Conversely, the *anti-hero* is a flawed character. Having chosen poorly in life, and most likely still choosing so, (s)he endeavors to do the right thing when doing the wrong thing would be more natural and even advantageous at times. Unlike the hero, who fights for others, the anti-hero struggles for his/her soul by helping others.

As mentioned earlier in this book, a peculiar change took place in the 1990s. In previous decades, the hero worked with law enforcement. However, as programs, like D.A.R.E. (Drug Abuse Resistance Education), brought in SROs (school resource officers) for the first time; we started seeing a massive uptick in juvenile arrests as our nation was ironically facing a dramatic downturn in violent juvenile crimes.

Both Democrats and Republicans had created a silent, joint war on our nation's youth. Where poor performers, in a school, would be arrested, and tried as adults, for innocuous offenses, no adult would ever be charged with a felony and misdemeanor offenses. These juveniles would be scurried off by SROs before testing could commence – hence artificially hedging the school's state grading to maximize funding.

As a result, at the height of the comic book market's golden era of publishing, law enforcement officers were seen by the juvenile audience as evil, while contemporary comic heroes were viewed as the supporters of an unjust, and even mad, society. The anti-hero soon rose to popularity with comics. Older comic anti-hero characters, mostly from the 1970s, who had almost fallen into obscurity, saw a massive upsurge during this time.

One could say, the traditional comic book industry of the 1990s was gutted by our new digital era. Poor youth can no longer easily buy comic books. Instead, one must purchase expensive graphic novels. The joy of a weekly, or monthly, childhood comic book purchase is now gone. The industry, in a sense, left their audience behind as they focused on new markets.

For this reason, hero and anti-hero stories have waffled in sales as major comic book players, like DC and Marvel, have turned to television and cinema to find new audiences. In doing so, they have cannibalized many characters, to make less violent works complying with parental guideline suggestions. They are also replacing many traditional stories with lesbian, transgendered, and other heroes they hope will appeal to a new, and previously untapped, demographic. Ironically, viewership and sales have indicated that these industry titans no longer know their audience base at all.

In adult works, heroes and anti-heroes are not as prevalent. If portrayed, it is generally a maverick in some banal profession or occupation, such as a rogue lawyer, a bullheaded doctor, a vigilante detective, or a troubled fireman with a death wish. More sophisticated, these works look greater at the human condition than grand concepts of altruism. Also, since adults do not have to be worried about being arrested for innocuous offenses, as children do, one does not see broad vacillations between hero and anti-hero consumption.

In truth, one could expect the same audience to pick up books on heroic doctors and soldiers just as easily as they would pick up books on anti-hero police officers, vengeful judges fighting the system, etc.

The Innocent/Sinless

To have an *(anti)hero*, or virtuous main character, there must be someone to fight for, or avenge the injury/death of, in a story.

Babies are considered the most innocent. As a person's age rises, and their gender made known to the audience, their level of innocence is significantly colored. Oft times, the viewer will perceive a general lack of purity just by these two considerations of age and gender. Sadly, even in contemporary society, another huge bias towards innocence is the race of the character.

However, this perceived lack of innocence is reclaimable by the *innocent*, or *sinless*, based purely upon their relationship with the (anti)hero or main character.

This interplay is exemplified in William Mark's *From Behind the Blue Line* where a police officer's son is abducted and made into a sex slave for various pedophiles. The officer risks his career, his marriage, etc. to bring his son home.

A far different example can be seen in *To Kill a Mockingbird* by Harper Lee. Here, the innocent person is a wrongly accused Black man. The only way the audience can see his innocence is by having a young, female, White child try to process the situation in her mind. Through her perceived innocence, the audience can see past any of their prejudices to discern the sinlessness of the man on trial.

Guru

We all need someone to turn to, who knows more than we do. We need a wise one who "knows things" and is willing to teach. They provide a transformative element because they represent the power of education and compassion, combined with the benefit of life experiences, to change and mold the future.

Because the audience rarely ever wants to be taught and lectured to, it'd greatly behoove the writer to incorporate some form of comic relief. It also doesn't hurt to have an antagonistic relationship between certain characters and the *guru*.

For example, in the *Firefly* franchise (2002-2005), Capt. Malcolm Reynolds (portrayed by Nathan Fillion) and Shepherd Book (portrayed by Ron Glass) often times had a somewhat rocky relationship. The Shepherd was a man of faith while Capt. Reynolds was a man of action – making for natural conflict to develop between the two. To cut tensions, Shepherd Book once suggested pedophiles, and people who talk in movie theatres will go to a special Hell.

If expressed outrage of the fans, concerning the short-lived nature of this franchise, is any indicator, one might also contend that there is a special Hell for screenwriters and movie executives for killing off many of the story's main characters – including Shepherd Book.

In *Kung Fu: The Legend Continues* (1993-1997), the dynamic was a bit different as the guru was also a father. Building upon a much earlier series, this spinoff sees the reincarnation of Kwai Chang Caine (portrayed by David Carradine) with his son, Peter (portrayed by Christopher Jay Potter). After a long separation, the father and son reunite in America where Peter is a cop and his father has a Chinese apothecary. Together, the two of them fight crime and forces of darkness. However, as with all father and son relationships, there are always tensions between the two – even if the father is a Shaolin monk able to enter Shambala at will.

To make the character more human, it never hurts to give the guru a hidden past or some mental ailment, or even an addiction; they must work through. However, many television shows have tanked because the guru took on the role of the main character and their flaws ultimately defined their motivations. Such heady works are generally going to be short-lived because it detracts from, rather than accentuating, a well-written story.

Like in contemporary American society, intelligence is not a valued commodity for most people to have. If anything, it can get a person into trouble. So, it is generally a wise idea to keep any guru character in the backdrop as a weak secondary, or even an exceptionally strong tertiary character to draw-in, and then quickly stash away from the storyline at will.

Twins

Sometimes referred to as *doppelgangers, twins* represent a duality in life between good and evil. Under rare exceptions, twins can represent pure evil. Part of this is due in part to C.S. Lewis' *Mere Christianity* where he contended that the *Devil* sent evil to humankind in pairs to separate and divide us. Therefore, some twin-based stories often involve confusion and working people against each other.

As of late, more and more stories are bringing back the old Romulus and Remus concept. Here, one twin is good and the other being either evil or troubled. An impending battle is to one day ensue where a twin, presumably the bad/flawed twin, will kill the other.

Occasionally, a story will use real-life twin stories to give an almost metaphysical element to a work. For instance, Elvis Presley had a twin who died. This led to an unfounded belief, among some in popular culture, that his talent was attributable to his deceased twin somehow metaphysically giving him double talent. Following this line of thought, some works operate upon the belief that certain powers, abilities, or traits are somehow passed along metaphysically to a surviving twin.

In other cases, we now know twins can absorb the other twin while they are fetuses in the womb. Such real-life examples often reveal how a person, later in life, might have a mass containing their incorporated twin. So, writers will generally take this and incorporate it into the story to have the absorbed twin take over the mind and body of its sibling host in the hopes of being birthed.

These latter, real-life cases, are often depicted in fantastical fiction to serve as an allegory for hidden family histories, adoption, divorce, family secrets, etc.

Scapegoat/Whipping Boy/Sacrificial Lamb

In life, there are multitudes of people who wrongly endure hardships for other, more affluent individuals. Sometimes, they are the ones who go to jail. Other times, these are the people who must routinely suffer financial, mental, and even physical abuse because of some "untouchable" person. These characters represent a significant aspect of the human condition concerning socio-economic classes. Through the character's sufferings, we see the humanity in them.

Sid Fleischman's book, *The Whipping Boy*, masterfully explains to children this concept. They are taught that if you endure hardships, you can still win out and become elevated yourself.

In adult works, there oft times is not a happy ending. Generally, the *scapegoat*, or *whipping boy*, rarely comes out the better for enduring their hardships.

Unique to the Appalachian Mountains region, it is not uncommon to have stories where a disabled person, usually with a mental disability, suffers tragedy to the point of becoming, an albeit tainted, *sacrificial lamb* so others might find peace and happiness amongst each other.

In the 2012 television series, *Hatfields & McCoys*, this type of age-old mountain story depicts where Anderson "Devil Anse" Hatfield (portrayed by Kevin Costner), and Randall McCoy (portrayed by Bill Paxton), start a family feud. As the show concludes, it was Devil Anse, allowing the hanging of Ellison "Cotton Top" Mounts (portrayed by Noel Fisher), which really ended the feud.

Regarding contemporary television and cinematic works, the scapegoat rarely has much allegory attached to it. Ironically, such a written-in plot diversion is usually used to get rid of a character's actor who is permanently leaving the set for health or other reasons. Thus, it is a way of honoring the actor, and therefore the character, by making them into a virtuous, sacrificial lamb either by death, incarceration, exile, or unemployment. An excellent example of the latter is seen in the *Spin City* (1996-2002) television series when Michael J. Fox, playing the role of Deputy Mayor Mike Flaherty, left the show due to Parkinson's disease.

Villain/Predator

The *villain*, or *predator*, is a person who seeks to rob people of their power, control, and authority. Sometimes, this is through petty property crimes. Other times, the price is murder. At the one end of the spectrum, these people are nothing more than damaged souls with no obvious solutions out of a life of crime. However, at the other end of the spectrum, these are dangerous creatures who are barely recognizable as humans.

In literature, cinema, and even in the sciences, there's a belief that predators are smarter and more cunning than their prey. Therefore, super intelligent villains commonly are portrayed as sexually-driven creatures who enjoy "the hunt."

Because villains and predators inherently represent a loss of power by others, they naturally embody victimization allegories, which cause the audience to detest these bad guys as rabid animals or bugs in need of extermination. Adult works may try to change this beast. However, in most cases, the audience wants the monster "put down."

Serial killers and serial rapists are particularly dark figures, which can create an intriguing storyline. It makes things even more compelling if the monster in the story is charming and personable; essentially forcing the audience to see the villain not as a monster, but rather as a person. Often this concept, contemplated in the 2016 movie *Jack the Ripper*, takes an iconic serial killer and asks what happens when the prime suspect is your sibling.

Explorer

Humans develop through our exploration. We do it as children in taking our first steps. We also do it as a society by deciding to build ships, fly like birds, or even build vessels to escape the hold of Earth's gravity.

Even here, there are various levels of exploration the crafty writer can utilize. In doing this, it is helpful to keep in mind the old business axiom, "Pioneers get shot; settlers get rich." The same is true for this type of plot.

We see this with the short-lived *Firefly* television and movie franchise. One of the few space operas where the originators chose not to portray alien cultures in space, all forms of character allegory were blatantly human. On the show, the viewers were carried from planet to planet by a rag-tag crew of for-hire explorers. Through portrayed interactions, the audience was able to see how humankind reacted to a given set of circumstances. As the resulting movie proved the old axiom true, nearly all the major stars of the show were killed trying to save humanity.

Explorer archetypes frequently represent both wisdom and the seeking of knowledge. The characters are dynamic and oft times flawed. While it is okay to have a singular person portrayed in an explorer story, it is best to have an assortment of characters working together. The more flawed, compartmentalized, and secretive these characters are – the better for creating various sub-plots and plot twists in the story. After all, these people are at the same time running towards something just as much as they are running from something.

Through this flawed perspective, the writer is better able to infer humankind's basic sense of curiosity and the ramifications for taking missteps in our pursuit of learning about the world around us. Thus, the audience is just "going along for the ride."

Healer/Fixer

Helping others is an amiable attribute. It indeed takes a special breed of person to be a *healer* or a *fixer* of problems. If this person is Black, a woman, someone who is disabled, etc., the situation can be made even more difficult – depending upon the era of the story. This is because not all people/patients want help and not all fixers/healers can save someone. This flawed dynamic, considering the dire odds and other, sometimes draconian, situations can lead healers to be especially enduring and endearing.

Healers and fixers generally are portrayed as horrible liars. For instance, the phrase "you might experience some minor discomfort" means they would be on a morphine drip if it were them. This is possibly a way for them to cope with sometimes difficult patients/people. However, the ability to tell a good lie effectively has been used in the past with great success. Key to the success of the lie is a belief that it is necessary in order to keep people, if not society, safe.

Believing they know what is best for people, they can be haughty. Better educated than the masses, they must fight not only their peers, but also the ignorance of the masses. This character, probably more so than any other, is defined as much by his/her story's era as the situation at hand.

In the *Dr. Quinn Medicine Woman* franchise (1993-1999), a female doctor had to fight ignorant men and less-trained peers in the classic American Old West. In contrast, *Gray's Anatomy* (2005-Present) deals with a female doctor trying to work her way up in a male-dominated profession while also experiencing the sensual pleasures of an independent, contemporary woman.

Sometimes, the healer/fixer isn't even a traditional medical expert, but instead someone who fixes a given situation or societal anomy based upon a different field of study or under-standing. For example, like with Dr. Quinn, the *Doctor Who* series marries-in the explorer plot type with the healer/fixer, to where a time-traveling alien/human hybrid works with humans to fix anomalies in the timeline. This is similarly true for the *DC's Legends of Tomorrow* (2016-Present), a series which uses human superheroes rather than an alien hybrid to time travel.

Conversely, the show, *Bull (2016-Present)*, uses a very flawed trial scientist, Dr. Jason Bull (portrayed by Michael Weatherly), and his team, to exploit humankind's own biases and psycho-logical traps in order to vindicate the innocent and bring justice to the guilty – despite an onerous, and oft times faulted, legal system.

The key element of developing a great healer/fixer charac-ter is to have someone who is just as flawed as they are helpful. People don't want to read, or watch, a story where everything is cloyingly perfect. But, at the same time, there also needs to be this keen desire to help, to make things right, to strive to save the little guy. In a sense, it is an elevation of the human condition to be noble.

Oppressed Soul

Whether the person is in jail, a slave, or under a dictatorship; the *oppressed soul* archetype talks to our unconscious mind regarding the issues trampled personal freedoms. Nothing is more pitiful than the innocent one in jail. Even the reformed convict, serving a life sentence, tugs at our hearts since we inherently want good people to be free. Stephen King exemplified this concept in his novel, *The Green Mile*.

In a country that has a history of killing and shipping off people to prison merely because of their ethnicity, incarcerating adults and children at a rate so steep, we now have "million dollar blocks," prison corporations now being openly traded on the stock market, and a government which can now legally surveil everything one does or says – this is the fodder for works steeped in the oppressed soul archetype.

It is a warning for us to stop and remember certain axioms of our society, such as, "Innocent until proven guilty." Because, by the grace of God, it could be us wrongly behind bars.

Hunter

Historically, the hunter was a provider of food and furs. He was a noble and respectable person who was depended upon during dark times.

Today, hunting has become somewhat of a taboo topic. Therefore, the contemporary hunter seeks other men as prey in pieces using a detective, vigilante, or other such characters to track down "bad guys."

This allegory is essential because it strikes our inner desire to see justice exacted upon those who attack the weak and innocent.

Still, some writers use the old hunter character in their work in a different fashion. Here, the figure is rarely depicted favorably. Treated as someone not to be trusted, the hunter is regarded almost as a hermit or sociopath.

In some cases, the traditional hunter character is demonized even more by being made into a horrible demon or a vile alien creature. Regarding this allegorical concept, consider its usage by the *Predator* film series (1987-Present) where an alien species hunts human beings for sport. Here, the creature is used as a subconscious argument against the practice of hunting.

While indeed a touchy topic, it should be noted that most of the literary and cinematic world are oft times politically left-leaning in their beliefs. By this, I mean they hold political views where they oppose hunting and the owning of weapons by private individuals. They express their beliefs in their writing.

However, it is important to note, purely from a marketing and sales perspective, that there is a significant portion of our nation, geographically speaking, which happens to be right-leaning in their political views. In truth, only major cities tend to have populations with political opinions, which are congruent with the beliefs of industry creators. Thus, there is a vast, and untapped market waiting for the portrayal of the hunter archetype utilized with a positive connotation.

Who knows, maybe one day the hunter archetype could be portrayed as intelligent, patient, persistent, and benevolent with an overriding desire to provide and protect. The niche market is there for anyone wishing to capitalize on it!

Lovers, The Femme Fatale & Sex Slaves

Oh, to love and be loved! But then again, maybe it isn't love at all, but rather lust, which drives man's beating heart. Either way, as any good marketer would attest, sex sells!

Often, unless written for a romantic piece, the *lovers* archetype is a distraction. Their actions and antics take other character's, and even audience's, attention away from the real issue(s) at hand – making it easier for the writer to manipulate the storyline.

Over the years, a specific subset of the lover archetype has emerged – the *femme fatale*. Less a diversionary character, and more of the main character, the femme fatale archetype is in a league like no other.

This mysterious and seductive woman can drive males crazy. Her hapless victims are often dragged into dangerous situations.

Often, she leaves a trail of dead lovers in her wake. And, despite men knowing all of this to be true, they ironically almost line up waiting to be her next victim.

One suggestion for this vixen's power is she serves as a historical, Christian fiction representation of where a churchless life can lead. She offers what should be in a marital relationship, but isn't, and then gives the penalty for chasing one's passions outside of the marriage.

Throughout history, the Christian Church has tried to regulate marital relations in one form or another – many times going against what the *Holy Bible* says on the subject. Specifically, despite indicating a marriage should have almost daily sex (1 Corinthians 7:3-5), and said marital relationship should involve a host of taboo actions ranging from seduction and oral sex to even masturbation in front of one's love (Song of Solomon 2), the truth is most Christian teachings have followers believing sex should be severely limited and highly restrained.

Starting around the 1800s, men began to leave the church, and even families, with increasing frequency. The phenomenon led American churches into a host of pro-feminine teachings, including, but not limited to, wives limiting sex in the relationship. Marital sex was eventually meant only for procreation and nothing else. To make matters worse, you had only one position condoned by church officials – ironically dubbed the "missionary position" and technically the only legally allowed position in Florida.

Being American culture did not publicly allow for mistresses, and given the churches' new stance on sex in the marriage, this left even more men secretly running to the arms of other, less churched, women who would fulfill their sexual needs. Thus, the femme fatale archetype grew ever-popular in Christian fiction and secular works until the early twenty-first century when divorce became popular and extramarital affairs no longer became such a taboo subject to engage in.

In this regard, one of the best examples of such an archetype is the 1992 film, *Basic Instinct*. Quite fittingly, the movie came out just after the massive divorce craze of the 1980s, when churches were raging against popular culture to save marriages.

In the movie, Catherine Tramell (portrayed by Sharon Stone) is a sexy, seductive, single novelist blamed for the death of a rock star. True to form, she has every guy's tongue hanging out in awe – even if she might be a violent killer. In her sights is Det. Nick Curran (portrayed by Michael Kirk Douglas), who she easily seduces into a steamy relationship. The story is further complicated by Det. Curran's psychologist, and lover, Dr. Beth Garner (portrayed by Jeanne Tripplehorn) being another possible suspect in the murder.

Lately, with church attendance falling at record rates, and the normalization of couples living together, and even having children, outside of wedlock; it should not be surprising to see femme fatale stories almost become non-existent in contemporary works. A Christian fiction archetype, the femme fatale is dependent upon a society that is in a terrible moral quandary between an extreme, perceived need to be virtuous and a carnal desire to meet specific basic needs that one often cannot find in the marriage.

While not a lover, the *sex slave* is an archetypal character which falls in and out of favor. In a way, it is the opposite of a femme fatale.

In 1985, when the Christian Church was much, much stronger than it is today, Margaret Atwood penned *The Handmaid's Tale*. Now a hit television series (2017-Present), of the same name, the story depicts Christians taking over America, forming their own country of Gilead, and creating a caste system which includes sex slaves known as "handmaids." The reason for the sex slaves is because most of North America has gone sterile! Ironically, Atwood pulled from the *Holy Bible* an obscure passage, only really being found in a handful of versions, telling how a couple used a handmaiden to act as a surrogate mother (Ruth 3:1-3 King James Version, New American Standard Version, et al.). In other words, a single passage became fodder that she then used in her anti-Christian, dystopian piece to let the sex slave serve as an allegory for religious oppression, the dangers of intermarrying church and state matters, and the devaluing of women.

Polymath

A *polymath* (a.k.a., *Renaissance Man, Universal Man,* or *Homo Universalis*) is a cultural anomaly holding a comprehensive knowledge on a wealth of subjects including, but not limited to: math, science, literature, music, and art.

There are periods in history where humanity is on the brink of chaos, and it is the multi-faceted polymath which saves everyone from destruction. Much of Europe would still be in the Dark Ages had it not been for the polymaths of the Renaissance Era. America would still be colonies had it not been for polymaths such as Jefferson and Franklin. And, it was Nikola Tesla, who ushered America into a new era of science and innovation by giving us many of our modern-day luxuries such as the radio, the screw-in light bulb, alternating electrical current generators, electric cars, remote control devices, and more.

However, because a polymath commands such a varied array of topics, and can combine seemingly unrelated concepts, they are scorned and made to feel dejected by society when things aren't on the brink of collapse. Because of this, writers usually depict this archetypal character as either suffering from a mental illness, an addict trying to dull the mind, a sex-crazed fiend, etc.

The allegory of the *polymath*, or *universal man*, archetype is merely a person who is so fully self-aware and educated; (s)he has reached the pinnacle of human evolution. However, because polymaths are rare, finding someone to understand them is difficult. It is even harder for them to find a mate which fulfills their every need.

Examples of polymaths in literature and television abound. However, most writers prefer to use the Sherlock Holmes character to represent the ideal of this archetype.

Stephanie Osborn's *Displaced Detective* series of novels brings Sherlock Holmes to a version of contemporary society where he finds his soul mate in a female scientist. Meanwhile, in the *Elementary* television series (2012-Present), the storyline is set in today's world with the major players existing in our contemporary society.

The tragic element of a polymath is that society cannot appreciate the brilliance they hold. To mix art and science into a singular concept is nothing more than madness for many. So, for the writer wishing to use such a character, one should consider putting the polymath in a story situation where they excel – society at the brink of chaos. Maybe it is the pending Second Civil War of America, or it might be humanity's pioneering of new planets. Whatever the storyline's setting is, make the needs of the other characters so great they will suspend their prejudices to embrace any solutions the mad polymath might bring forth.

Epilogue

By now, you've realized the subject of archetypes and allegory is as varied as the faceted points of light on a large diamond. They come together, diverge, color, and contrast in nuanced ways to fit the needs of the storyline and the hidden innuendo sought by the storyteller.

Even minor tweaks in the description of the character can have a significant impact. For instance, do you want to depict someone who is fiery and resolute? Make the character into a redhead! Do you wish to make the character to be lazy and a dullard? Then make the character obese. Writing about an older character can make them appear wise while writing about a younger character can make them look brash.

In these cases, nothing changes with the storyline so much as our own biases are coloring how we perceive the characters in the finished work.

Sometimes, the archetype's allegory is varied. In other instances, it can be deeply entrenched. This is important to note how the sales of final works, and even future spinoff of said works, are made and broken just by how the writer attributes a given allegory to the archetype.

Yes, applying the wrong allegory to the wrong archetype can be disastrous. However, just as harmful to the storyteller is when they do not take into account cultural viewpoints regarding the portrayed archetype and allegory. While great regional story-telling may take place using local archetypes, sales tend to lose steam once the work hits audiences outside of the targeted demographic.

There is nothing more valuable to a storyteller than a command of iconic archetypes and the allegories they represent. It is vital to stay ever-vigilant in observing how other works use certain characters in given situations. One must look to see what is selling, what is not, and especially what is experiencing an anomaly in sales and interest. These anomalies, more than anything, will tell you what is working, what isn't working, and also clue you into possible aspects others may not have yet recognized.

About the Author

Ken Johnson is a culturalist (a.k.a., Social Scientist), conflict specialist, business consultant, artist, and a multiple award-winning author. He routinely writes and lectures on issues of culture and conflict. When not writing and lecturing, Ken loves attending cultural events, cooking, outdoor sports, and feather painting. He also serves on numerous non-profit and professional boards. In 2005, the Governor of Kentucky commissioned Ken as a Colonel. Later, in 2018, the Florida Authors and Publishers Association honored him with their most prestigious award possible, the Founders Award. Presently, Ken Johnson lives in Northwest Florida with his wife, Toshana. They have three little dogs which Ken calls his "editors" for their propensity to mess with his keyboard when wanting his attention.

Group Discounts for
A Quick Guide to Archetypes & Allegory
ORDER FORM

Use this form to order *A Quick Guide to Archetypes & Allegory* by Ken Johnson for the groups you are a part of or may know. Bulk order discounts apply. Please feel free to photocopy this page as many times as is needed for ordering more books.

The following discounts apply:

2-25 Copies	$6.26 each (a 10% discount)
26-50 Copies	$5.56 each (a 20% discount)
51-100 Copies	$4.87 each (a 30% discount)
>100 Copies	$4.17 each (a 40% discount)

Prices subject to change

Quantity	Price Per Book	Total
_____	@ $ _____	$ _____
	7.5% FL Sales Tax	$ _____
	Shipping & Handling Fee	$ _____
	$10 or 10% (Whichever is greater) for US orders; $20 or 30% (Whichever is greater) for Overseas orders	
	GRAND TOTAL	$ _____

Billing Information
Name: _____

Address: _____

Phone Number: (_____) _____ - _____

Email: _____

Shipping Information
Name: _____

Address: _____

Mail Cashier's Check or Money Order (Made payable in US Funds) to:

Heritage House Books
P.O. Box 263
Milton, FL 32572

CPSIA information can be obtained
at www.ICGtesting.com
Printed in the USA
FSHW021732150719
60033FS